A Cloudy with

of Meatballs Cookbook

Flint Lockwood Diatonic Super Mutating Dynamic Food
Replicator

BY - Sharon Powell

License Notes

Table of Contents

Introduction

Do you actually love Cloudy with a Chance of Meatballs? Do you want to throw the ultimate food party for your kids? Are you looking for simple recipes that your kids can learn? You have come to the right place!

Flint Lockwood creates the ultimate food machine known as the Flint Lockwood Diatonic Super Mutating Dynamic Food Replicator or FLDSMDFR. A welcome change from baby sardines that the town consumes.

Flint and Sam embark on various journeys in the two movies often revolving around food. The second instalment introduces us to Foodimals, who are food shaped animals.

This book consists of 30 easy recipes that your kids will love to make. Call their friends over and surprise them with these delectable, easy-to-make recipes.

Let's start!

Chapter 1: Drinks to Get the Party Started!

1. Fruit Cockatiel

Foodimals are adorable food shaped animals. Each one has unique characteristics based on fruits and vegetables. Fruit cockatiels have pear bodies with pineapple eyes, banana legs and orange hands. Here is a simple cocktail recipe your kids will love to make.

Serving size: 4-5

Cooking time: 20 minutes

Ingredients:

- 1 cup Greek yogurt
- ½ cup fresh cream
- 1 teaspoon vanilla extract
- 1 mango, chopped
- 1 bunch grapes, deseeded
- 2 tablespoons honey
- 1 cup strawberries, chopped
- 2 oranges, chopped
- 1 apple, chopped
- 2 bananas, chopped
- 2 tablespoons dry fruits (almonds, raisins, cashews)

Instructions:

1. Add cream, yogurt, honey and vanilla to a bowl and beat till stiff peaks form.

2. Refrigerate for 30 minutes.

3. Next, add all the fruits to a blender and whizz till smooth.

4. Mix it with the yogurt and serve with dry fruits scattered on top.

2. Cantaloupe

Cantaloupe is an amphibian with a large cantaloupe body and seeds for teeth.

Serving size: 2

Cooking time: 10 minutes

Ingredients:

- 1 cup vanilla yogurt
- ½ cup cantaloupe, chopped
- Ice cubes
- 1 cup orange juice

Instructions:

1. Add yogurt, cantaloupes, orange juice and ice cubes to a blender and whizz till smooth.

3. Kiwi Smoothie

Kiwis resemble Kiwi birds from New Zealand except they look like kiwi fruits. They are often spotted on top of other Foodimals trying to pick insects.

Serving size: 2

Cooking time: 5 minutes

Ingredients:

- 4 kiwis, peeled and chopped
- 1 mango, chopped
- 2 cups pineapple juice
- 1 banana, chopped

Instructions:

1. Add kiwi, banana and mango to a blender and whizz till smooth.

2. Pour in the pineapple juice and mix.

3. Serve cold.

4. Flamango

Flamangos look like flamingos with mangoes for face and body. They love socializing with each other and flocking together.

Serving size: 2

Cooking time: 10 minutes

Ingredients:

- 1 large mango, chopped
- 1 tablespoon honey
- 2 cups cold water
- Mint leaves

Instructions:

1. Add mango, water and honey to a blender and whizz till smooth.

2. Serve cold with a mint leaf on top.

5. Barries

Apart from foodimals, there are sapient food beings that look like fruits but possess human characteristics. Barries are large strawberries who are easily scared and excrete strawberry jam when they feel anxious.

Serving size: 4-5

Cooking time: 10 minutes

Ingredients:

- 1 cup strawberries, chopped
- ½ cup raspberries, chopped
- 2 cups vanilla yogurt
- 3 teaspoons jam
- ½ cup milk

Instructions:

1. Add strawberries, raspberries and yogurt to a blender and whizz until smooth.

2. Add to a pitcher and pour milk and mix.

3. Add jam and mix till combined.

4. Serve cold.

Chapter 2: Starters and Main Course

6. Spaghetti Meatballs

Of course, meatballs. The basic theme of the movie. Don't we all wish we had a machine that could drop delicious meatballs from the sky?

Serving size: 6-8

Cooking time: 40 minutes

Ingredients:

- ½ lb pork mince
- 5 tablespoons oregano
- 5 tablespoons basil
- 2 teaspoons sugar
- 1 onion, chopped
- 2 eggs
- 1 onion, chopped
- ½ cup breadcrumbs
- 2 paprika, chopped
- 1 cup tomatoes, pureed
- 1 tablespoon garlic, minced
- 2 tablespoons Tabasco sauce
- 2 cups spaghetti, cooked
- Salt and pepper to taste

Instructions:

1. Add half onion, oregano, Tabasco, basil, sugar, pork mince and breadcrumbs to a bowl and mix till well combined.

2. Season it and shape into meatballs.

3. Next, place on greased baking tray and bake in a 375 Fahrenheit oven for 20 minutes or until soft inside and crispy outside.

4. Then, add oil to a pan along with onions and garlic and brown.

5. Add tomatoes, paprika, salt and pepper and mix till combined.

6. Toss in the spaghetti and mix till combined.

7. Add to a plate and add 2-3 meatballs and parmesan cheese on top and serve.

7. Wild Scallions

Foodimals are a big part of the movie and some of the best characters in the series. Wild scallions are tall scallions modelled after giraffes and dinosaurs.

Serving size: 6

Cooking time: 45 minutes

Ingredients:

- 5 large scallions
- 1 tablespoon olive oil
- 1 large potato, chopped
- 5 cups chicken broth
- ½ cup cream
- 2 tablespoon butter
- Salt and pepper to taste

Instructions:

1. Add butter and oil to a pan along with scallions and brown.

2. Toss in potatoes, chicken broth, salt and pepper and mix.

3. Simmer and cook till potatoes are soft.

4. Next, add to a blender and whizz till smooth.

5. Pour into bowls and add a tablespoon of cream on top and serve.

8. Eggplanatee

Eggplanatee are creatures that look and behave like manatees with eggplants as their bodies. Your children will fall in love with eggplants after they try this recipe.

Serving size: 4

Cooking time: 30 minutes

Ingredients:

- 1 large eggplant
- 5 tablespoons milk
- 1 cup breadcrumbs
- 1 ounce parmesan cheese
- 1 tablespoon basil leaves
- 2 cups marinara sauce
- 3 ounces mozzarella cheese
- 1 egg

Instructions:

1. Add milk, eggs and pepper to a bowl and mix.

2. Add breadcrumbs, basil and parmesan cheese to a plate and mix.

3. Cut the eggplants into half and dip it first in the egg mixture followed by the breadcrumb mixture and place on a baking dish.

4. Bake in a preheated 350 Fahrenheit oven for 45 minutes or until its soft.

5. Sprinkle mozzarella on top and bake for 5 minutes.

6. Serve warm.

9. Sasquash

The Sasquash or big food is a play on the famous bigfoot. Just like the original, sasquash is an elusive creature with strange interests such as jogging on the beach and standing on balconies without views.

Serving size: 2

Cooking time: 30 minutes

Ingredients:

- 2 lb butternut squash
- 1 tablespoon butter
- 1 tablespoon olive oil
- 2 tablespoons honey
- Salt and pepper to taste

Instructions:

1. Add the squash to a baking tray and bake in a 400 Fahrenheit oven for 30 minutes or until soft.

2. Once cool, cut it into squares.

3. Next, add them to a bowl along with butter, oil, honey and salt and mix.

4. Add it back to the baking tray and bake in a preheated 400 Fahrenheit oven for 30 minutes.

5. Serve warm.

10. Shrimpanzees

Shrimpanzees look like chimpanzees but with shrimps for limbs. They swing from tree to tree and are friendly creatures.

Serving size: 7

Cooking time: 10 minutes

Ingredients:

- 14 shrimp, deveined
- 2 tablespoons soy sauce
- 2 teaspoons honey
- 1 tablespoon oil

Instructions:

1. Add honey, soy sauce and oil to a bowl and mix.

2. Add the shrimp and marinate for 20 minutes.

3. Add oil to a pan and sauté the prawns till cooked.

4. Serve warm.

11. Mosquitoast

Mosquitoes can be extremely annoying, but Mosquitoasts are super cute! They have a toast for wings and raisins for eyes. They prey on Buttoads.

Serving size: 8

Cooking time: 20 minutes

Ingredients:

- 8 bread slices, toasted
- 1 cup pizza sauce
- 2 cups mozzarella cheese
- 1 teaspoon oregano
- Salami

Instructions:

1. Add toast to a baking tray and place bread slices over it.

2. Apply pizza sauce and sprinkle cheese and oregano on top.

3. Add salami and bake in a preheated 375 Fahrenheit oven for 20 minutes.

4. Serve warm.

12. Wildabeet

Wildabeets have purple beetroot bodies with bushy leafy tails and roots for noses. They are spotted swimming or running around the jungle.

Serving size: 5-6

Cooking time: 10 minutes

Ingredients:

- 5 beetroot
- 2 tablespoons oil
- Salt and pepper to taste

Instructions:

1. Clean and peel the beetroots and cut them into slices.

2. Add them to a baking tray and drizzle oil all over.

3. Sprinkle salt and pepper and bake in a preheated 425 Fahrenheit oven for 20 minutes.

4. Serve warm.

13. Meatbalrus

The Meatbalrus has a meatball body and breadsticks for front teeth. They are strong and heavy creatures used to destroy things like cars.

Serving size: 4-6

Cooking time: 30 minutes

Ingredients:

- ½ cup carrots, chopped
- ½ cup parsley, chopped
- 1 onion, chopped
- ½ cup breadcrumbs
- 1 lb beef mince
- 2 tablespoons milk
- Salt and pepper to taste
- ½ cup parmesan cheese

Instructions:

1. Add carrots, onion, parsley, beef, breadcrumbs, salt, pepper, parsley and milk to a bowl and mix till well combined.

2. Press the mixture down into a bread tin and bake in a preheated 400 Fahrenheit oven for 30 minutes.

3. Slice and serve with marinara sauce.

14. Tomato Soup

Tomatoes are chubby red tomatoes with small beady eyes. They are rarely seen and aren't happy creatures, except for a few. Here is a simple tomato soup recipe that your kids will enjoy making and eating.

Serving size: 2

Cooking time: 30 minutes

Ingredients:

- 4 tablespoons butter
- 1 onion, wedged
- 1 cup tomatoes, chopped
- 2 cups vegetable stock
- Salt and pepper to taste

Instructions:

1. Add butter and onions to a pan along with tomatoes, salt and pepper and simmer.

2. Pour stock and cook until soft.

3. Add to a blender. Then, whizz till smooth.

4. Serve warm.

15. Subwhale

Subwhales are aquatic animals with a sub sandwich body, lettuce leaves for flippers and tails, and olives for eyes. Despite being big, they are friendly creatures.

Serving size: 4

Cooking time: 20 minutes

Ingredients:

- 1 loaf bread of choice
- 4 cheese slices
- 4 turkey slices
- 4 lettuce leaves
- 1 small cucumber, sliced
- 1 large onion, sliced
- 1 large tomato, sliced
- 1 tablespoon jalapenos, sliced
- 1 tablespoon olives, sliced
- 2 teaspoons mustard
- 2 teaspoons mayonnaise
- 2 teaspoons ketchup
- Salt and pepper to taste

Instructions:

1. Add mustard, mayonnaise, ketchup, salt and pepper to a bowl and mix

2. Slice bread in half and apply the mixture on the inside.

3. Lay the lettuce leaves over it followed by turkey, tomato, onion, olives, jalapenos and cucumber slices.

4. Place the cheese slices over it and cover.

5. Slice into subs and serve.

16. Pearl Onions

Pearl onions look and act like dogs. They are like chihuahuas and carried around by lady pickles.

Serving size: 4

Cooking time: 15 minutes

Ingredients:

- ½ lb pearl onions, trimmed
- 5 tablespoons olive oil
- 1 lb lettuce, chopped
- 2 tablespoons vinegar
- 2 tablespoons chives, trimmed
- 1 tablespoon tarragon, chopped
- 1 tablespoon basil, chopped
- Salt and pepper to taste

Instructions:

1. Add water and salt to a pan and toss in the onions.

2. Once soft add to a bowl along with salt, pepper, vinegar, chives, lettuce, basil and tarragon.

3. Mix and serve.

17. Pizza Giant

Pizza Giants are food people who live in foodimal jungle. They look like pepperoni pizzas with thin arms and legs. Your kids will actually fall in love with this simple and delicious pizza.

Serving size: 4

Cooking time: 45 minutes

Ingredients:

- 15 ounces pizza dough
- 25-30 pepperoni slices
- 12 ounces mozzarella cheese
- 1 teaspoon oregano
- Salt to taste

For sauce

- ½ cup tomato sauce
- ½ teaspoon sugar
- ½ teaspoon garlic, minced
- ½ teaspoon pepper flakes
- ½ onion, finely chopped
- 1 teaspoon olive oil
- Salt and pepper to taste

Instructions:

1. First, add oil to a pan and toss in garlic and onions and sauté till brown.

2. Add tomato sauce, salt, pepper, sugar and sauté till thick.

3. Roll the pizza dough to fit your baking pan and press it down.

4. Apply a layer of tomato sauce on top and sprinkle pepperoni slices, oregano and cheese.

5. Then, bake in a preheated 400 Fahrenheit oven for 30 minutes.

6. Slice and serve.

18. Hot Dog

Hot dogs appear on hoardings and have thin legs and hands. They wear white gloves and white shoes and have smiley faces. These hot dogs are sure to put a smile on your children's faces too!

Serving size: 6

Cooking time: 20 minutes

Ingredients:

- 6 grilled sausages
- 6 grilled brioche buns
- 6 tablespoons caramelized onions
- 4 tablespoons grilled corn
- 4 tablespoons green beans
- 4 tablespoons chives, chopped
- 3 tablespoons ketchup
- 3 tablespoons mustard
- 3 tablespoons ranch dressing
- Salt and pepper to taste

Instructions:

1. add ketchup, mustard, ranch dressing, salt and pepper to a bowl and mix.

2. Apply inside the buns and sprinkle onions, beans, corn, chives.

3. Add sausages and close the buns.

4. Serve.

19. Carrot Salad

Carrots are food people. They are upside down carrots with smiley faces and their leaves for legs. This healthy carrot salad is a good way to make your kids fall in love with carrots.

Serving size: 4

Cooking time: 20 minutes

Ingredients:

- 1 lb carrots, peeled and chopped
- 2 tablespoons parsley, chopped
- 2 tablespoons chives, chopped
- 1 cup chickpeas, cooked
- 2 tablespoons olive oil
- 2 tablespoons lemon juice
- 2 teaspoons honey
- 1 teaspoon mustard
- ¼ teaspoon cumin powder
- Salt and pepper to taste

Instructions:

1. Grate carrots and add to a bowl along with chives, parsley and chickpeas and mix.

2. Add honey, mustard, salt, pepper, lemon juice, olive oil and cumin and mix.

3. Add to the bowl and mix.

4. Serve and enjoy.

20. Pickle

Pickles are sapient foods that have formed their tribe. They are like humans and friendly. Here is a kid-friendly pickle that your kids can make and enjoy.

Serving size: 4

Cooking time: 1 hour

Ingredients:

- 3 cups vinegar
- 1 cup salt
- 4 quarts water
- 3 lb cucumbers
- 5 teaspoons pepper
- 5 fresh peppers, chopped
- 5 garlic cloves, minced
- 1 bunch dill leaves, chopped

Instructions:

1. First, boil water in a pot and add vinegar and salt.

2. Clean cucumbers and slice them.

3. Next, add to the water and cook till soft.

4. Sterilize 6 canning jars and fill them with the pickle.

5. Add equal quantities of pepper, hot pepper, garlic and dill into each jar.

6. Allow it to cool before refrigerating.

7. This pickle can last up to 2 weeks.

21. Buffaloaf

The Buffaloaf has a meatloaf for its body and is covered in ketchup. It has corn for teeth, onion rings as horns and parsley for hair.

Serving size: 4-6

Cooking time: 1 hour 20 minutes

Ingredients:

- ½ cup ketchup
- 2 tablespoons sugar
- 1 tablespoon Worcestershire sauce
- 1 onion, chopped
- 1 tablespoon garlic, minced
- 1 egg
- 1 tablespoon milk
- 2 lb beef, minced
- 1 teaspoon mustard
- 2 cups wheat cereal crisps
- Salt and pepper to taste

Instructions:

1. Add sugar, ketchup and mustard to a bowl and mix.

2. Add half to another bowl and add Worcestershire sauce, onion, garlic, salt, egg, milk, beef and pepper and mix till combined.

3. Add wheat cereal and mix.

4. Make small meatloaves using the mixture and place on a greased baking tray.

5. Next, bake in a preheated 350 Fahrenheit oven for an hour.

6. Apply the reserved sauce over each and bake for another 15 minutes.

7. Serve warm.

22. Cucumbird

Cucumbirds look like birds and have a long cucumber for their body and quartered cucumbers for their wings. They travel around the island in small flocks. Here is a fun carving activity your kids will love.

Serving size: 2

Cooking time: 10 minutes

Ingredients:

- 1 large cucumber
- 1 small cucumber
- 2 cloves

Instructions:

1. Slice the large cucumber halfway. Make sure you don't go all the way.

2. Pierce the cloves through the top to make eyes.

3. Quarter the small cucumber and attach it on either side of the large cucumber using toothpicks.

23. Hippotatomus

The Hippotatomus is a large potato-shaped foodimal with a butter pad for tongue and chives for teeth. They are happy go lucky creatures who are territorial.

Serving size: 4

Cooking time: 20 minutes

Ingredients:

- 12 baby potatoes
- 4 slices turkey bacon, chopped
- 1 broccoli bunch
- 1 tablespoon olive oil
- 1 cup cheese, shredded
- Salt and pepper to taste

Instructions:

1. Wash potatoes and pierce with a fork.

2. Next, place on a greased tray and bake in a preheated 325 Fahrenheit oven for an hour or until soft.

3. Slice them in half and add back to the tray.

4. Boil broccoli in boiling water until soft and add over the potatoes.

5. Add turkey bacon, cheese, oil, salt and pepper and bake at 400 Fahrenheit for 10 minutes.

6. Serve warm.

24. Tacodile Supreme

A tacodile supreme is like a crocodile with a taco for its body. It plays an important role in Cloudy with a Chance of Meatballs 2.

Serving size: 5-6

Cooking time: 20 minutes

Ingredients:

- 2 tablespoons oil
- 1 onion, chopped
- 2 cups sweet potato, chopped
- 1 lb beef mince
- 10-12 taco shells
- 3 corns, husks removed
- ½ lb cherry tomatoes, halved
- 2 cucumbers, sliced
- 1 baby lettuce, shredded
- 2 cups cheese, grated
- 2 tablespoons taco seasoning

Instructions:

1. Add oil, onions, sweet potatoes, salt and pepper to a pan and cook for 5 minutes.

2. Add beef and vegetables and sauté.

3. Add taco seasoning, corn and water and cook till beef is soft.

4. Place the tortillas on a plate and sprinkle beef, cucumber, corn, lettuce, tomatoes and cheese.

5. Serve warm.

25. Susheep

Susheep are sushi shaped Foodimals that have sushi rolls for their bodies and act like sheep. They are fun-loving and gentle creatures.

Serving size: 4

Cooking time: 30 minutes

Ingredients:

- 2 cups sushi rice
- 2 tablespoons rice vinegar
- 1 tablespoon sugar
- 1 cucumber, sliced
- 1 avocado, sliced
- 1 carrot, sliced
- 2 eggs, sliced
- 4 nori sheets
- 2 tablespoons mayonnaise
- 2 tablespoons soy sauce
- Salt and pepper to taste

Instructions:

1. Wash rice and boil till soft.

2. Next, add vinegar and sugar to a saucepan and bring to a boil.

3. Pour over rice and mix.

4. Mash the rice till soft.

5. Place nori sheets on bamboo mats and add a tablespoon of rice over the edge.

6. Place carrots or cucumbers or eggs or avocados and roll tightly.

7. Mix mayonnaise, soy sauce, salt and pepper and mix.

8. Cut and serve with the dip.

Chapter 3: Desserts

26. Watermelophant

Watermelophants look like elephants with watermelon bodies. They have slices carved out to make their mouth. They have roots as trunks and leaves as ears.

Serving size: 4

Cooking time: 5 hours

Ingredients:

- Half watermelon, cubed
- 4 kiwis, chopped

Instructions:

1. Add watermelon and kiwi slices to a blender and whizz till smooth.

2. Pour into popsicle molds. Then, freeze for 4 to 5 hours.

3. Serve cold.

27. Apple Pie-thon

The apple pie-thon is a very interesting foodimal. It has a slice of apple pie as its face with cinnamon sticks as its tongue. Its body is made of a giant piece of Twizzler and has vanilla ice cream on its head.

Serving size: 4

Cooking time: 15 minutes

Ingredients:

- 1 small apple pie, 4 slices
- Twizzlers
- 4 scoops vanilla ice cream
- Cinnamon sticks

Instructions:

1. Place apple pie slices on 4 plates.

2. Insert one end of the Twizzler into the bottom of the pie and curl the rest.

3. Insert cinnamon sticks to make teeth.

4. Add then a scoop of vanilla ice cream on top of the pie.

5. Apple pie-thon is ready!

28. Marshmallow

Marshmallows are living food species with a cylindrical marshmallow for their bodies and tiny black eyes and mouth. They are always smiling and happy creatures. Your kids will actually be super excited to try out this marshmallow recipe.

Serving size: 4

Cooking time: 1 hour

Ingredients:

- 3 tablespoons gelatin powder
- 2/3 cup syrup
- 2 cup fine sugar
- 2 tablespoons vanilla essence
- ¼ teaspoon salt
- Pink gel food color
- 1 cup water
- 2/3 icing sugar
- 2/3 cup cornflour

Instructions:

1. Add gelatin and ½ cup water to a bowl and mix.

2. To a double boiler add sugar, remaining water and corn syrup and mix.

3. Add cornflour and icing sugar to a large bowl and mix.

4. Once the sugar boils gradually add the gelatin and mix.

5. Stir till it turns thick.

6. Add salt and food color and mix till combined.

7. Add vanilla and mix.

8. Dust a tray with half the sugar and cornflour mixture and pour the marshmallow over it.

9. Allow it to set for 20 minutes.

10. Dust the remaining flour mixture on top and cut it into slabs.

29. Lemmins

Lemmins are lemmings with a lemon body. They have beads for eyes and pout for a mouth.

Serving size: 4

Cooking time: 30 minutes

Ingredients:

- 1 cup rolled oats
- 3 tablespoons flour
- 2 teaspoons baking powder
- 1 tablespoon butter, melted
- 1 small egg
- 2 tablespoons honey
- 1 lemon, juice and zest
- 5 tablespoons desiccated coconut

Instructions:

1. Add oats, flour, baking powder and desiccated coconut to a bowl and mix.

2. Add butter, eggs, lemon juice, zest and honey to another bowl and mix.

3. Mix the two until well combined.

4. Add a tablespoon of the mixture on a greased baking tray and bake at 350 Fahrenheit for 15 minutes.

5. Cool and serve.

30. Peanut Butter and Jellyfish

Peanut butter and jellyfish have peanut butter toasts as their bodies. They are lovely delicious!

Serving size: 1

Cooking time: 10 minutes

Ingredients:

- 2 bread slices
- 2 tablespoons jam
- 2 tablespoons peanut butter

Instructions:

1. Toast the bread slices.

2. Mix the peanut butter and jam and spread it over the toast.

3. Cut diagonally and serve.

Conclusion

There you have it. 30 delicious recipes your kids will fall in love with! You can inspire them to take up cooking as a hobby.

Feel free to mix up the ingredients. Help your kids create unique signature dishes.

Go on, watch as your kids cook up a storm in the kitchen!

About the Author

As a child, spending time in the kitchen excited Sharon. She particularly enjoyed her family ritual of cooking together during the weekends, but she didn't think that would be her path. Actually, at the time, she thought she could only be a chef or own a restaurant and wasn't sure if she could pull it off.

She spent most of her mid-20s in a cubicle at an advertising agency where she worked as a copywriter. At every chance she got, she let herself dream and pen down cooking ideas, which she would experiment with and try to create whenever she got the chance.

She wanted more as her yearning for food cultures grew. After a eureka moment, she figured out that she didn't have to be a chef or own a restaurant before she did what had always been a part of her. She did some research and found out a catering school where she earned a diploma.

Deciding to write as much as she can about food, she took up part-time editor roles at food blogs and also ghostwrote a couple of cookbooks before she branched out to do her thing.

She resigned her job and turned her home, which she shared with her fiancé to her office. A decade later, she shares it with her husband, their two kids, and a dog, and she is still writing about food.

Author's Afterthoughts

Perhaps, one of the greatest fears a writer has is to be the author of a book no one reads. This fear lingers for so long that it takes a lot to shake it off – if you shake it off. So, you must know how thankful I am to you, my reader that you went for this book and read it. Believe me, it is a dream come true.

We have connected with this book, and I would like for us to stay connected. I would like to hear your thoughts about the book, and I am sure there others who are waiting for comments such as yours to decide if this book is the right fit for them. If you enjoyed reading this book and learned something from it, (I hope you did) I would like to ask you to leave a review. I hope that it is not too much trouble.

My sincerest thanks,

Sharon Powell

Made in the USA
Monee, IL
04 September 2021